Body Language, Intuition & Leadership!

Surviving Primary School

By: Orly Katz

Illustrations: zofit shalom

Thank you for purchasing this book!

It is very important to me to get your feedback and hear what you think!

Please write a review on Amazon and let me know your thoughts.

Table of Contents:

Introduction

Dear Readers,

I want to congratulate you on your decision to take action and learn how to survive Junior High by joining me in this, the third book of the series!

In each of the four books in the series we discover new keys which together unlock the secret of being 'Simply Me' and together teach you how to believe in yourself and gain self confidence and self esteem.

Anyone in primary school knows just how tough it is to:

-Know what to do with your hand, to decide where to look and exactly how to stand when the teacher calls you up to the front to address the whole class...and everyone is staring straight at you...

-Try to impress the best looking kid in the class, when instead of talking...nothing comes out of your mouth, you go red and stare at your feet...

-Make decisions about what to do...and who to mix with...and to understand what signals your body is sending when you get goose bumps or feel faint...

I've got great news for you; it really doesn't have to be like that...

Things don't have to be so hard.

Imagine that you have a secret key "The Key to Body Talk" which shows you:

-The secrets of body language which the popular kids and class leaders already know!

-How to radiate self confidence, even when you're not saying anything, just using body language...

-How to listen to what your body is telling you and to understand your intuition which helps you make the decisions that are best for you!

This book, the third in the series, will help you learn a great many things that are really important in primary school that no class teacher tells you about. You will discover:

The secret that the popular kids already know: how to project charisma and leadership through body language

Most importantly you'll learn how to be "simply me" and to survive primary school...

Back in the eighties I was in exactly the same situation that you are now...in primary school.

-I didn't believe in myself, I was shy, I used to stand to one side and stare down at my feet...

-I ignored what my body was trying to tell me and didn't recognize any of my intuitions

-I mixed with the wrong people who I didn't feel comfortable and didn't have any true friends...

Until I decided that all this simply had to STOP! I understood that my body knew best what was right for me and I could use my intuition to help me decide who I should mix with and who I should stay away from...and when I changed my body language my social status improved too!

In this book you'll find a lot of true stories about things that happened to me when I was your age...

And if I succeeded in getting through it all, anyone can!

So how will we do all of this?

As well as true stories, there are helpful tips and fun exercises, quizzes and questionnaires and your own personal journal which you can use to test exactly where you stand in different areas....

I recommend that you don't try to fool anyone when you read the book and fill in the questionnaires and your journal, especially not yourselves.

Answer the questions honestly-there are no wrong or right answers everything is right...

So ...don't you want to start reading?

So, without waiting any more time, let's get started.

Are you ready?
Good luck!
I hope you'll
enjoy it,

orly

The Key to – Body Talk

This Key helps us to listen to what our body is trying to tell us, to recognize our intuitions which usually point us in the right direction. This is also the Key to understanding body language.

A True Story- The Six Million Dollar Man

When I was at school back in the eighties we didn't have parties for the whole year and we didn't have internet we just had class get-togethers at the youth club once a month on Friday nights. I want to tell you what happened at one of these get-togethers.

I used to get excited for the whole week before the class get-together. I would plan what to wear, think about who would be there, decide what I was going to say...

I can still remember the clothes I had decided to wear that particular evening after deliberating over my choice for hours. I had picked a knee length denim skirt, we didn't wear short mini-skirts back then like girls do today; and a cheese cloth shirt.

We had decided that we would meet in the playground outside the youth centre.

Now I should explain that in those days there were only two or three television channels and almost everyone watched exactly the same programs.

One of the most popular programs back then was 'Steve Austin -The Six Million Dollar Man' which was screened early on Friday evenings. Steve Austin was an astronaut who had been mortally wounded and then 'rebuilt' at a cost of six million dollars. He has new engineered legs, a bionic right arm and left eye which give him super human strength and special powers that help him carry out his missions. He was as strong as superman and used his strength and his ability to see to great distances using his bionic eye to fight crime.

The whole class would watch the latest episode before coming to the get together. We all knew that as soon as we met we'd start talking about the latest escapades of Steve Austin, the bionic man.

We all turned up as planned at the playground outside the youth centre, having watched what had been an especially exciting episode. It gradually got dark and perhaps because we were excited by the program we'd just seen or perhaps because the oncoming darkness created an atmosphere of mystery, some of us noticed that one of the lights was on in the top floor of the youth centre. It was supposed to be empty and none of us had gone in there yet. All the windows were dark except for the one at the end of the top floor. Everything that I'm going to tell you actually happened extremely quickly but try to imagine it in slow motion.

Mike turned to me, looked deep into my eyes, grabbed hold of my hand and said with a winning smile "Orly, come with me to the top floor, we'll go to investigate what's happening, there may be burglars up there...."

And I... very simply ...fell in love.

I fell in love with Mike. Mike wasn't the best looking boy in the class, but he was funny and apparently brave too. My heart started beating like a drum, I felt a warm wave flow through me and it was just as well that it was dark because I'm certain that I had blushed and turned as red as a beetroot. Mike had turned into my own personal Steve Austin. I knew that, in spite of my fears that there really were burglars in the local youth centre at 7pm on a Friday evening, that I would follow Michael to the ends of the earth come what may.

I could still feel the touch of his hand on mine from when he had asked me to climb after him, into the 'lion's den'...

We climbed the stairs bending over forwards, keeping our heads down; with the rest of the class following close on our heels, and decided to take cover before peering through the window of the door of the room with the light on. Mike was up front, I was close behind him, completely unaware of what was going on, while all the rest of the class was behind me.

Mike peeped into the room and saw...nothing. It was just the youth centre. Mike tried to open the door with me standing straight behind him, but it was locked. One of the Youth Leaders must have forgotten to turn the light off. All the same we had enjoyed being Steve Austen, fighting crime, if only for a moment.

I went home that evening feeling like I was floating on a cloud. I asked myself whether this is how you feel when you fall in love, and just could not calm down. I thought that taking a hot shower may help me relax, and in the shower under the stream of hot water surrounded by steam I carved Michael's name into the bar of soap. I stood staring at his name in the soap. Then I realized that everyone would see what I'd done when they came to take a shower in the morning so I spent ages rubbing his name off the soap. That night I only thought about Mike and I wondered whether he was thinking about me too.

I thought he was...

Needless to say the weekend took forever. All I wanted was for it to be 8.30am on Monday morning so I could meet Michael.

I got up early on Monday to make sure that I looked as pretty as possible and spent ages planning what I'd say. Then just before class started I saw Mike. I was scared that everyone could hear my heart beat; I was scared that everyone could see straight through me and knew exactly what I was feeling. I ran up to Mike, looked deep into his eyes and all that came out of my mouth was "What time is it?"

After all of the nervous energy I'd put into planning everything, after all of my hopes and dreams all I'd been able to say was "What time is it"! Mike answered me "It's half past eight" and that was it.

For one whole year I was secretly in love with Mike, he was my first love...and I never told him.

So why am I telling you this story about Mike now?

Because my body had been talking to me; telling me things. My heart was beating. I had blushed and turned as red as a beetroot, I was flustered, I couldn't sleep, I couldn't stop thinking about Mike. I listened to what my body was telling me:"You are in love..."

This is the power of the Key to body talk. Through the Key to body talk we learn that we can listen to the things that our bodies are telling us, and so understand our true feelings. Our body can send us messages through good, pleasant feelings and through less pleasant feelings and we can gain a lot by listening to these feelings and acting accordingly

The Rule for Intuition

Our intuitions help us to decide what we
should and should not do; what is right
for us and what is wrong for us; who we
should spend time with and who we
should not spend time with. Once we
learn to interpret our intuitions and to
understand what our body is trying to
tell us, we feel amazing!

Our body sends us messages in the form of different feelings. We have to recognize what each feeling means to understand what our body is telling us. For instance if we feel nausea and stabbing sensations in our chests we probably don't want to be involved with whatever is making us feel that way.

When we follow our heart and inner feelings we become much happier.

The Rule for Good Feelings

If by chance you are experiencing any of the following

- A floating feeling
- Palpitations or butterflies in your stomach
- A strong circulation
- Giddiness
- Rapid heat beat
- Rapid breathing

Then you are probably receiving the signal "This is great"

The Rule for Less Pleasant Feelings

If by chance you are feeling any of the following

- An annoying headache
- A dry mouth
- Nausea
- Stomach Ache
- Perspiration
- Pressure
- A thumping feeling in your chest from your heart
- Stabbing feelings in your chest

Your body is probably warning you "stay away".

A True Story - The Note

When I was at school we needed a special pass to leave the school during school hours. We called that pass 'the note'.

This story took place towards the end of the Christmas term when all the Christmas lights were already up in the centre of town and everyone was thinking more about parties and Christmas presents than school. That particular year the shops were having one –day pre Christmas sales as well as the normal January sales to try to get even more people to buy things. Those sales were calling out to us, with special offers on everything we dreamed of buying or receiving for Christmas presents, but we knew that if we waited until school was over most of the things we wanted may be sold out.

It was Marty who had the idea first.

He told Shelley and she told Peter who told me. I told Claire and she told Sarah...and in that way we slowly put together the following plan.

We decided that Peter and Shelley would go to the secretary's office together and 'swipe' six of the notes from on her table.

The plan was quite detailed. Shelley would distract the attention of the secretary by asking her all sorts of questions while Pete sneaked the notes off the table being careful not to be seen.

The next stage was that Sarah, who had beautiful handwriting and who could forge our teacher's signature, would fill in the details on the notes and then sign our teacher's name on each one of them.

I didn't have a special role to play but I was still part of the plan and my stomach had started to hurt from the moment we had begun to discuss the idea.

I felt that something was really, even terribly wrong.

We put our plan into action during the first recess. Peter and Shelley went into the secretary's office and five minutes later came out with broad grins spread across their faces and the 'loot' in their hands.

When Pete handed the notes over to Sarah so she could forge our teacher's signature I felt as though hammers were knocking on the inside of my head. What did I do about all these things I was feeling? Nothing!

Sarah forged the signatures on the notes with incredible skill and handed us the notes. We had signed passes!

Everything had gone smoothly, perhaps too smoothly. We had the signed notes in our hands and the six of us set off together in the middle of the morning out through the school gates. Where were we headed? To the sales of course.

The gatekeeper glanced at the notes…

Everything was in order. Nothing should have made him suspicious. Then however he made one little comment, a comment that made all of us change colors, going from normal color to bright red, then to white and then silenced us so we all turned dumb.

"It's rather unusual that all of you are all being allowed out of school all together in the morning. Where are you six headed to?"

There was a blank silence and no-one opened their mouths.

We'd messed up...badly. We hadn't planned on anyone asking us where we were going. Normally when someone left school the gatekeeper looked at the note and that was it.

"Umm. Err we're um going to our voluntary work project" Marty mumbled with his eyes fixed to the ground his head bent forwards and with a terrible stutter.

Perhaps it was because the way we had been changing color with a display good enough to shame your average chameleon, or because our body language was letting on that all we wanted to do was vanish into thin air.

We hadn't made much of an impression on the gatekeeper and he decided to take action. He took hold of the passes looked at them again and again and then rang the school secretary who connected him directly to our teacher.

The ending...you really don't want to know. We were severely punished. Letters were sent to our parents and warnings given as to the consequences of any further slip ups. It was altogether an unpleasant experience. We did apologize and tried to explain that it was the end of term, the Christmas spirit and all the advertising of the sales that had distracted us, and that we'd slipped up just that once, but nothing helped. They were extremely strict and severe with us.

My own conclusion-I should have listened to my own intuition, to the messages my body was trying to send me with those headaches and stomach pains (intuitions are also called gut feelings...apparently there's a good reason for that).

Why had I ignored the banging pains in my head and the horrendous stomach ache I'd experienced?

I didn't want to be the odd one out. I didn't want to be any different to anyone else and I didn't want to spoil all of the fun. I didn't want to be the only one who wasn't cool and I didn't know how to stand up for myself.

I suppressed everything that I was experiencing and tried to push all my feelings to one side. I paid a heavy price for ignoring what my own body was trying to tell me.

Do you listen to your intuition?

Circle the answer which best fits how you would behave in each one of the following situations, and then add up your scores.

Situation	Answers				
	Definitely not	Probably not	Maybe	Probably	Definitely
Someone in your class asks you out and you think that you could be good together, but all your friends tell you that you are not right for each other. Would you stop going out with them?	1	2	3	4	5
You went to a party and your friends started going wild,	1	2	3	4	5

breaking things and messing up the house. You're not part of it but your friends start saying that whoever doesn't join in is a nerd. Would you join in?					
You meet a new group of friends and go into town with them to see a film and eat pizza, but you don't really get on with any of this new group. Would you go out with them again?	1	2	3	4	5
You have a new hobby, which you really enjoy and which you're good at. Your	1	2	3	4	5

friends tell you that it's really babyish. Would you give up your new hobby?					
Someone you've met on 'Facebook' invites you to their house, but you have a bad feeling and think that it's a set up, and they aren't who they are pretending to be. Would you go to meet them anyway?	1	2	3	4	5

The analysis

5-11

Good for you! You follow what your heart tells you and make wonderful use of your intuitions and know how to listen to your feelings. You don't latch on to other people or get caught up in things. You know what's good for you and are not scared of acknowledging it. Keep on going!

12-18

You are aware of your instincts and intuitions and know what your heart is telling you to do, but don't always have the courage to do it. When you do follow your instincts you feel terrific. On other occasions you're not quite so sure of yourself and prefer to settle for doing what everyone else is doing. Try to practice listening to your own intuitions. You'll discover that it really does work for you and the more you practice the better you'll feel. Good luck!

19-25

Any connection between what you do and what your intuition tells you to do occurs completely and utterly by chance. You try to bury your own feelings somewhere deep inside of you and don't pay any attention to them. It's social pressure that counts for you...and that's a shame. Remember we're not talking exact science here, we're talking about feelings, but usually our own intuitions aren't wrong.

As we have seen it's important to keep in touch with our feelings and our intuitions and our bodies can help us do that. But our bodies can help us in other ways.

We all share one common, international language which isn't taught in school but is the most useful language you can learn. This language tells the world everything you can't or don't put into words. It's body language!

Through a tremendous variety of expressions and gestures our body language spills the beans on those things we so often try to hide with our words.

A True Story - The Unusual Witness

This next story took place in a courtroom and it includes a kind of detective challenge for you. Let's see if you can solve it...

As you know it is the jury which decides whether a defendant is guilty or innocent in trials. In this particular trial the defendant facing the jury was charged with murder.

The trial was almost over, but the jury was completely mystified as to whether the defendant was guilty or not. They simply did not have the slightest idea. The trial had failed to recreate what had happened and no-one, including the judge, seemed to have formed a clear idea as to whether the defendant was guilty or not.

At that point the judge decided to take matters into his own hands and to surprise everyone present in the courtroom. He stood up and announced that in about one minute the murdered man was going to walk into the courtroom.

All of the jurors turned their heads and looked expectantly towards the door waiting to witness the unfolding drama. They waited for one minute and then for another one before looking back at the judge who announced that his summing up of the trial was now concluded and that they could retire to the jury room for their deliberations until they had reached a verdict.

The jurors went into the jury room and five minutes later came out again.

The judge turned to them and asked if they had reached a verdict. They responded that they had, and that it was unanimous.

"What is your decision?"

"Guilty"

After the trial the jurors were asked what had made them reach their verdict so quickly.

At this point I am stopping the story and will ask you the same question. What made the jury members return a unanimous guilty verdict?

This was the answer:

"When the judge announced that the murdered man was going to enter the courtroom everyone in the room looked at the door, everyone except for one person, the defendant. He knew that the murdered man couldn't walk through the door!"

The lesson we learn from this story: This is the power of body language. Our body language communicates all kinds of messages, often sub consciously, and gives away all sorts of things about us, but also helps us understand all sorts of things about the people around us.

The First Rule about Body Language

We can practice using movements, postures and tones of voice to project the messages we want to give to those around us.

A True Story- Charisma

Jonathan joined our class in the middle of one school term. Most children who joined a class midway through the school year took time to settle in and make friends but Jonathan was different.

Jonathan was not particularly good looking, he wasn't a great athlete or particularly good at school work, but he had something more important than all of those put together. Jonathan was a born leader. He had great self confidence and was extremely charismatic, attracting people to him.

The way he talked, the way he stood, the way he returned people's looks straight back to them and his full happy laughter all made people want to be around him. They wanted to enjoy his company and they wanted to follow him... through fire and water. Jonathan wasn't afraid of saying what he thought, he wasn't afraid of expressing himself even when his opinions were different to those held by the majority. He simply was "Simply Me".

The story I'm going to tell you took place during a school camping trip towards the end of the school year.

This trip was organized so that the whole class could spend the night together in a huge tent at a camp site. We all had sleeping bags, and had been waiting until we arrived at the camp site so the real fun could begin.

Our campsite was at the bottom of a mountain and quite a strong wind blew through the valley. Our tent was fairly weather proof, except near the flaps where people could come in and out. Once the tent was ready for us everyone started to position their sleeping bags. Some saved a place for a friend; others made sure they slept in a particular position (or at least found somewhere where they thought they might sleep during the night...)

Then Angela came into the tent...

This is where I should explain to you about Angela, who was one of the most popular girls in the class, but unlike Jonathan who people followed because they wanted to, Angela held her position by terror...everyone had to do what she said...or else.

Angela walked into the tent holding her sleeping bag, looked around until her eyes settled on Karen who was lying down next to Lauren who was one of Angela's sidekicks. Without batting an eyelid Angela said to Karen:

"Take all of your stuff now and move to by the tent flap. I don't want to sleep by the flaps and besides, Lauren is my friend, I want to sleep next to her."

Excuse me!!! I was shocked.

Had I heard right? What right had Angela to order
Karen about?

Why should Karen move her things and go to sleep near
the entrance to the tent where it was windy and cold?

That was Angela's problem...

All those thoughts went through my head but I didn't
say anything, I just carried on watching what was
happening.

A few more girls joined in, following on after Angela,
telling Karen that she had to move immediately.

Karen didn't answer but just curled up where she was, and didn't move.

It was then that I saw Jonathan at his best. He got up and stood straight to his full height, and looked directly at Angela and said something I have always remembered.

"Angela, collect your things and go and sleep by the entrance to the tent. You came last. Karen doesn't have to move anywhere!"

Believe it or not, Angela collected her things, and laid out her sleeping bag near the flap of the tent, without saying another word.

This is the power of leadership and charisma. This is the power that self confidence and confident body language have. Jonathan was charismatic. He had self confidence and carried us all along after him without exception. Do you want to know what Jonathan did, and what you can do to give off an aura of self confidence?

The Second Rule about Body Language for Self Confidence

What should we do to project self confidence?

-Stand up straight without slouching

-Look straight at the eyes of the person opposite you

-Keep your arms hanging freely with out clenching your fists or crossing your arms

-Smile from your heart with laughter in your eyes

-Speak fluently without pausing or stuttering or saying er or um.

-Direct your body towards the person you are talking to
-Keep a suitable distance between yourself and the person you are talking to

Going back to our story, that is exactly what Jonathan did.

He stood straight, looked directly at Angela, didn't get flustered; spoke fluently, without stuttering or pausing, without shouting, and calmly achieved what he wanted to. Angela left Karen alone and went to sleep by the tent flap herself.

Do you take advantage of people?

Draw a circle round the answer which best suits each situation for you and then add up your score...

	Definitely not	Probably not	Perhaps	Probably	Definitely
You know that the biggest geek in the class is also a mathematical genius. Would you pretend to be friends with him just so he's help you study for exams?	1	2	3	4	5
Your younger sister has done your regular babysitting job for you while you went out with friends? Would you keep most of the money and give her less than half of the sum?	1	2	3	4	5
Someone in your class has a fantastically good looking brother/sister. Would you become friends with them	1	2	3	4	5

just to get a date?					
One of the wealthier kids in the class invites their close friends round to see movies on their home cinema. Would you suck up to them just to be invited?	1	2	3	4	5
The kid next door, who goes to your school, gets a car for his 17th birthday. You aren't friends but would you try to become friends just to get lifts to school?					

The Analysis

5-11:

You're aware of other people's feelings and try not to take advantage of people. That's great. However, it's actually not so bad just occasionally to ask for something small from people who aren't your close friends.

12-18:

You know the difference between taking advantage and asking for small things. You're not too shy or too pushy. Keep it up.

19-25:

Manipulation and taking the advantage are your second names! Try to think how you can get by without taking advantage of people.

And the conclusion is... Charismatic children who are natural leaders don't need to take advantage of people to get what they want. Everything they do radiates confidence and their body language does too. That alone is enough to get the whole class to follow them.

Writing about Myself-
Worksheets:
The Key to Body Language

1. <u>Positive and negative physical sensations:</u>

Write down one occasion when you experienced a positive physical sensation. (For example floating, butterflies in your stomach, hearing bells chime...)

1. What exactly happened

_____

_____

_____

2. What did you feel?

_____

_____

_____

3. What can be concluded from that?

_____

_____

_____

Write down one occasion when you experienced a negative physical sensation. (For example nausea, trembling, stomach ache...)

1. What exactly happened?

_____

_____

_____

2. What did you feel?

_____

_____

_____

3. What can be concluded from that?

_____

_____

_____

2. <u>My Intuition:</u>

When was the last time that you followed your intuition?

1. What happened?

_____

_____

_____

2. How was your intuition expressed? How did you feel about the experience?

_____

_____

_____

3. In what way did you follow your intuition?

_____

_____

_____

4. What was the result?

_____

_____

_____

3. What stresses you out?

1. What causes you to feel stressed? (Parents, school work, friends)

_____

_____

_____

2. What physical sensations do you experience when you feel stressed?

_____

_____

_____

3. How does stress affect you?

_____

_____

_____

4. Body Language

Either watch a friend while they are delivering a speech, or look at yourself in the mirror while you are practicing giving a speech, and fill in the table.

	Movements, positioning, characteristics
Palms of Hands	
Central Body	
Arms	
Standing Still/ Pacing	
Standing straight / Slouching	
Fluent speech / Stuttering and hesitating	
Distance from the audience	

Facial Expression	
Eye contact	
Smiles	

The conclusions:

Most people are nervous about standing in front of an audience. One of the reasons for this is that they don't know how to make their body language work for them. We can practice and improve our body language. Being aware of what we are doing is the first step in the right direction.

5. Listening:

Practice giving your full attention and really listening to the person talking to you for one week (Brothers and sisters, friends, parents, teachers)

1. Did you find it difficult to pay attention to what you were listening to?

    _____

    _____

    _____

2. Did you succeed in really listening?

    _____

    _____

    _____

3. How did you achieve that?

    _____

    _____

    _____

We can't finish without a short summary...

Dear friends,

We've come to the end of this part of our journey towards 'discovering myself'. I wanted to thank you for coming along for the ride, so together we could make some important discoveries on that important question 'how can we survive primary school?'

This is the third in the series of books which together can help you learn those things that are really important to know in primary school and practice them until they become second nature. It explains those things that you've always wondered about, and wanted to know, but class teachers just don't explain.

This book has introduced you to 'the key to body talk' which has let you into the following secrets:

-How the popular kids and class leaders use their body language.

-How to radiate self confidence, even when you're not saying anything, just using body language...

-How to listen to what your body is telling you and to understand your intuition which helps you make the decisions that are best for you!

Now it is time to get to work and start practicing listening to your body talk and using your body language.

By using this key which is so, so simple you can feel happy, contented, satisfied, charming, beautiful, rich, wonderful, clever, cool, popular, loved, amazing, admired, hypnotizing, awesome, astounding, brilliant, cute, charismatic, hot, wicked, cool dudes, positive, friendly, sought after, sexy and everything else....

Seriously now:

Using this Key will help you to simply be you...who you really are and to feel good about yourselves and with what you want and with the things you do.

All I have left to say is that I hope you enjoyed reading this as much as I enjoyed writing it.

Now...it's time to get busy... so .get started putting everything you have learnt into practice!

Wishing you
all things
good,

orly

Thank you for purchasing this book!

It is very important to me to get your feedback and hear what you think!

Please write a review on Amazon and let me know your thoughts.

About Orly Katz:

Mother, author, lecturer, facilitator, young at heart, full of love, curiosity, and passionate about her work:

• Expert on child and youth empowerment.

• Co-Founder of "Simply Me International", an educational company, which provides accredited online courses for teachers and focuses on Leadership, Empowerment, and Self-Esteem.

• Author of numerous books on Amazon:

  ○ The "Simply Me" Series
     (for Teachers, Parents and Educators)

  ○ The Surviving Junior High / Surviving Primary -Series

  ○ Busy Dizzy (for ages 4-8)

  ○ The Princess Who Wanted a Friend (for ages 4-8)

• Lives in Haifa with her husband and three children.

For more information about Orly's work:

www.SimplyMeInternational.com

Other Books By Orly Katz:

Surviving Primary School

Surviving Junior High

Busy Dizzy
for ages 4-8

The Princess
Who Wanted a Friend
for ages 4-8

Other Books By Orly Katz:

The "Simply Me" Series

(For Teachers, Parents, Therapists & Coaches)

The Card Games Kit:
(For Teachers, Parents, Therapists & Coaches)

Made in the USA
Middletown, DE
09 November 2021

52005895R10040